LETTERS TO THE HOME

poems

by Michael Gray Bulla

Cover photo from the author's personal collection.
Illustrations by Michael Gray Bulla

PAB-0609-0292 • ISBN: 978-1-4867-1799-6

ABOUT SOUTHERN WORD

Through the literary and performing arts, Southern Word offers creative solutions for youth to build literacy and presentation skills, reconnect to their education and lives, and act as leaders in the improvement of their communities. Southern Word has grown to be a national, non-profit leader in the youth literary arts field, serving more than 7,500 youth, 67 schools, and 12 Tennessee counties last year. From guiding and hearing the stories of tens of thousands of youth, Southern Word understands our society's shortcomings as they relate to youth engagement, literacy, diversity, and mental health.

Learn more at www.southernword.org

This book is made possible through the support of the Nashville Mayor's Office, Metro Arts: Nashville Office of Arts + Culture, Nashville Public Library's Studio NPL, Nashville Public Library Foundation, and Urban Word.

CONTENTS

PART I

THIS IS HOW THE WORLD ENDS

i.
I am sitting on the porch and the world / is burning around me.
The porch swing creaks / where I rock it and I just keep rocking
it, / and the world is burning around me, the sky turned to cement
and the air is thick / with death and smoke and Armageddon, and
I / am sitting on the porch. The door is open. / I am sitting on the
porch. My feet do not touch / the ground when I swing, and I don't
hear it / when my family calls for me to *come inside, / please, just
come / inside.*

ii.
I am sitting at a desk with a sketchbook in front of me / and I am
drawing like I will die if I do not. This morning / the whole school
stood for the Pledge of Allegiance and / I was still drawing and
I am sitting at a desk and I am still / drawing. I will die if I do
not. I woke this morning feeling / the earth twist underneath me,
preparing for something, / something, and now I need to prepare
myself for this, / the only way I know how.

iii.
I am sitting in a car and the world has not prepared itself / for
this great fissure, a quick slice straight down the middle / like
the universe took a switchblade to its malleable body, and / I am
sitting in the car and my mother is in the front seat and / my
sister is next to her and I am listening to them speak / as I wait
for the apocalypse to come, / for fire to rain down to the earth and
send the whole planet up in / flames.

iv.
I am sitting on the floor and the world is not burning but / I wish
to god it was because at least then everyone would know / what
happened. I am sitting on the floor and my knees dig / into the
carpet and I have never cried so hard / and I wish the world was
ending ending ending / because at least then all eight billion / of
us tiny creatures would be mourning, / instead of only me and
seven others— / sorry. Six.

v.
I am sitting on the porch and the world / is still not burning and
my family / does not ask me to come inside. / The porch swing /
creaks when I rock it and I / just keep rocking and rocking and /
rocking and rocking / and rocking.

A LETTER TO THE HOME

It was your staircase that did it; the way you
slept so quietly. I cut my thumb on the shower door
and had a dream I fell down down down and busted
my head open at the bottom of your stairs. I bled and

you sleep. You sleep. You sleep. How many secrets
do you keep locked inside closets? You keep them so well.
Who glued your mouth shut, and how can I unhinge
your jaw until you spill out the history I

have sought out for years? You sleep so deeply,
your light bulbs flicker when you dream and you dream

so often.

CELLBLOCK

My dad won't talk about it.
I never visited her there. No one would let me.
In my dreams it looked like a hospital room,
smelled the same. In my dreams she slept
without a blanket and made friends with her cellmate.
In my dreams I was allowed there. In my dreams she
wore orange and told me she loved me. In my dreams
she served a life sentence.

She does that when I'm awake, too.

BATTERY

My mom's car died twice the other day
in the middle of the road. A light flickered on
and it wouldn't start. Cars sped impatiently
around us, their steel bodies flying while we sat
unmoving, unflinching.
I wondered if anyone would hit us.

We'd known the car was broken for weeks
and never did anything to fix it. We didn't have
the time, the money. Instead, we put up with
sitting there, flashers screaming warnings,
the possibility of getting hit always there,
instead of fixing what we knew wouldn't work.

NEON

I was never scared to drive with her but
maybe I should have been. She had a million cars,
one for each life she lived, each boy who screwed
her over, each scar on her arm.
I only remember her Jeep.
She liked her boyfriend's motorcycle better.
How long did it take for that one to go too?

Sometimes, if I get up late at night, at that time between
the living and the dead, I can see the headlights of her car
staring at me from outside the window
as if waiting for me to come to her.

SHOTGUN

The light turns yellow. The car accelerates.
She kisses her fingers and presses them to the ceiling;
I mimic her from the passenger seat.

I'm still mimicking her.

A LETTER FROM THE YOUNGEST CHILD TO THE MIDDLE ABOUT THE OLDEST

We spent our childhoods afraid of something
we couldn't name. We wasted our days
singing on swing sets and our nights huddled in
trembling piles, limbs wrapped around each other
like the tighter we held on, the less danger we were in.
Your eyes were so brown, and hers so blue;
they looked like they held all the secrets to living
in them, but I wouldn't find out the reason for that
until years later.

The strangest things bother me now. Everything
bothers me now. I can't turn on the TV without seeing her
there, her face. Every reporter wears a ponytail and
every actress's eyes shine so blue next to mine. I think
about the picture hanging on the fridge.
How alive she looked, how alive she didn't. On Halloween
someone showed me a picture of a child's body and
I felt my own collapsing under—something, maybe,
memories, or the weight of living when she—

Isn't that funny? How everything affects me like that?
I can't speak about her without feeling like the world
is ending. I can't admit that she's gone without floating out
of my own body, watching my mouth move like I've got hooks
pulling at the corners of my lips. The stairs creak
under the weight of our father's grief. Twenty-nine months ago,
our house fell into a coma and I don't know when it'll wake up.

While it sleeps, I am only here,
hooks scraping close to my teeth
and stretching my mouth into something
gruesome.

But I am a child again;
we are children again, fresh from eight hours
of third and sixth grade, clutching each other while
outside our windows flash red and blue. The police car's
scream rings in my ears for months after,
the way our mother's voice does on nights
when she sings us to sleep.
Will it be okay? I'll whisper.
You'll tell me everything will be fine, but I
will be old enough then to realize when it is
I'm being lied to for my own
good.

These hooks tug at my cheeks even
now. Have you noticed the bleeding?
The punctures in my skin?

SWOLLEN

The image of my mother screaming is burned
into the backs of my eyelids, a hot iron
in the shape of a woman bowing into
herself, her arms twisted like branches with
grief. She backed away and into my aunt's

arms, saying the body in front of her wasn't
her daughter, demanding they show her her
daughter. It is the only time I have ever seen
her like that. I still have not healed from that
memory. I don't know that I ever will.

When I don't try to think about something else,
my mind always comes back to this: her voice,
her sobbing. Her despair. My father cradling me
like he is afraid someone will take me away, too.
Her eyes were closed. She did not look like

herself.

ETHER

She burned her heart out.
I say this because
it is a prettier way to present
the truth.

I call her a hurricane but she
was more like a wild fire.
I used to wonder if heaven
could see her smoke from
here.

Now I wonder where
the smoke comes from
at all.

BONE

I woke up the 11th with a cavity in my chest
that has been there ever since. That space will

be empty until the day my body rots into
earth, and even then I am worried it will be there,

a sister-shaped crevice, a slice into my sternum
that will remain even after I return to her.

SURGICAL

There's a reason I'm so scared of dissections.
They cut into her head. They moved her scalp.
Did they dig around in there? What did they find?
I feel sick just thinking about it; a thousand days
and I still feel sick. I don't think the nausea will ever
go away.

GRAPHIC

I keep thinking about the girl who hung herself
in a movie I watched the other day.
Her body didn't swing and that made it worse
somehow. Another jumped off a lighthouse.
Another pressed a gun to the roof of his mouth.
I keep thinking about the girl's bedroom curtain
swinging the way her body should have. I
read an article the other day about a father who
walked in on his daughter pointing a gun at herself.
She told him to turn around.

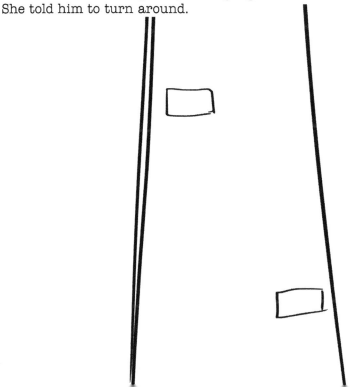

SLEEP TALKING

What am I trying to say?
Some part of me clicks
and whirs and looks for
the most important parts
to spit out.

I still can't find them.

DEADBEAT

I still don't know how to feel about him
or if I need to feel anything at all.
Does he deserve to be forgiven? Do I
have the right to forgive him?
It wasn't me he hurt.

Would she have? Had she already?
And if she had, does that mean I
should too? Being around him burns
nostalgia in my stomach and makes
me want to tie my feet to the floor.
I still don't know if that's good
or not.

SOMETIMES
WHEN I'M DOING WELL,

I fear that some vengefulness,
some storybook monster will drag
me back into a dark
I've since learned to forget
or at least to ignore.

I'm scared that it will clamp its spindly hands around my neck
and tell me that I have betrayed my sister in this way,
that I don't get to be happy when she's gone,
that unless I am sick I am not mourning.
How can you be so selfish? I'm afraid it will ask me.
How can you give yourself something she never got—
will no longer have a chance to get?

I don't know.

I wrote down every good thing that happened this year
and placed it in a Tupperware container.
I'm scared that this creature will use that against me,
will pull out the slips of memories as evidence that I
have forgotten her.

How will it use my happiness against me this time?
How much guilt will it place in that paper, waving it
around in the air like a sparkler?
Look at yourself, it will say. *You pathetic, selfish thing,*
and don't let yourself return
to something whole again.

COVET

I don't know if she was superstitious but this
bothers me more than it should. I want to know
everything:
her favorite flower.
What her cellmate looked like.
What she stared at when she was looking
through us.
I want it all.

Only after I cannot have it do I wish for it
so badly.

I flip through her photo album now, as if I could find
answers in the corner of her senior portrait, hoping it's
embedded in the withered flesh of her marriage certificate
or the drawings she did as a child. How did she like her coffee?

I wish only for answers
and maybe to forget why
I am asking for them so
late.

SMOTHER

How far did you walk the night you ran away?
I wrote so much about who you are.
The memory of you strangles me in my sleep
then teaches me to breathe again.

A POEM ABOUT GLASS

How many bottles did you smash before
you cut your hand? I want to know how
long it took to count the pieces. I want
to know how many of those you emptied
yourself and how much money you poured
down the drain.

I want to know what you named your first
car (and your second and your third and
your eighth) and if any of your heartbreaks
ever shared their names.

I want to know if flying through your
windshield felt the same as smashing
those bottles and if it did why you
would have ever stopped;

if the shards
stuck in your teeth tasted anything like
stepping bare-footed around the kitchen
floor;

if the red flashing of a police car
that night could ever compare to the
way the skin of your index finger split
open in slow motion, left alone to heal
itself.

Did the sweat drip into your eyes
that night, or did your vision blur
for something else?

Pick up the bottles
and try just to breathe.

AMPUTATION

I had a dream that someone sliced away the skin
and left my calf muscles open and raw. I didn't bleed.
I don't know if I was supposed to. I had a dream
that it didn't hurt. I'm scared it will. I'm scared
my hand will shake so much that my nails will
find a target they had lost for years now.

Sometimes
when I look at my legs
I see nothing.

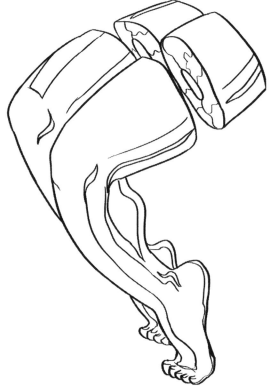

HOSPITAL

My niece still remembers the time I was
wheeled away in an ambulance. I wonder when
she will begin to ask why. When the answer
I was sick will stop being sufficient. When she
will put the pieces together. When she will no
longer be able to ignore that she knows nothing.
That we've kept everything.
How long until the kids at school ask? She
tells them easily her mother is gone. Past that,
I don't know what she says.

I WANT TO WRITE IN MEMORIES (PART I)

I don't cry anymore but I'm
not sure if that's a good thing.
If it stops hurting so much,
if it stops hurting so deeply,
if it stops hurting so often,
how do I know that it ever did?

What proof do I have but the words?
What proof do I have but
the past?

I want to write it all down so it can never
dissolve. So it can never dissipate from
my memory, can never leave me
alone
and bleeding. I want it here and I want it
alive,

but the white of this paper scares me,
and in the middle of my fear is the belief
that there will never be a way to get this
all down. That there are some things so
raw that they can never be recreated
in language,
and so they are left to rot only in flickering
screens and I,

I don't cry anymore.

EARTH, OR: A LETTER TO ANYONE WHO WILL LISTEN

When does it stop hurting?
The weight in my chest drags me down
like Atlas finally collapsing. How long do you
think he kept this up? Does it ever get
lighter?

Tell me if you can, please. I
don't know that my lungs will hold
under this for much
longer.

BIRDSONG

I swallowed a bird the other day and
have been coughing up feathers ever since.
I choked on its wing going down. I said,
this time it won't hurt, and I was wrong.
The bird said, *pay your price.* The bird
said, *you dug your grave,* and did not
have to tell me to lie in it. The other
day my bones rattled in my skin so
loudly I was afraid they would burst
right out of me. The other day I
didn't sleep. The other day I slept
too much. The other day the bird woke me
with its singing from my throat.
The other day, I sang for it.

Today, I contemplated getting in a wreck.
I turned the radio on for the first time
in months. I said, *just wait a few more
hours.* I said, *just hold out and you will
be fine,* and I didn't point out to myself
how I didn't add *safe.* Today, I lied to
myself. Today, I almost didn't. Today,
I went home thinking *I will be this way
forever.*

Today the bird did not sing from my throat, so,
when I got home, today, I swallowed another
just to see if it would sing.

MEMORY LOSS

The moment I am not with you I forget
we existed at the same time at all.

We occupied this space:

you, telling me a story, and me, laughing
when it is polite to. You, talking so easily,
and me, so harshly aware of every syllable
as it leaves my mouth, clumsy attempts at
self-awareness that toe the line of censorship
more days than not. This is the space we occupied:
you, natural; me, lying; me, hesitating;
me, trying; me, surviving,

                                 but this is not a survival story.

I walk the tightrope between us,
but this skill is one I have only just begun
learning while you have trained your entire life in it.
You watch me wobble and pinwheel to catch my balance,
watch me land with a thud on the days that I cannot
find my footing, and I wonder what you think of me.
How pathetic I must look, unable to speak without
breaking my ribs. How childish, how silly,
that I can't even do this right.

Even with a broken rib, I occupy this space with you.

But this is not a survival story.

So the moment we don't—the moment the tightrope
is folded into itself and placed far out of reach—
no amount of searching yields memories of what we
did. What we talked about. How exactly I got to this
ragged breathing.

I wonder who combed through my brain
and stole only the chunks and pieces where I am failing,
who wanted to erase the proof so badly.

I wonder if the falls haven't done something,

if my head hasn't taken damage
from one crash too many.

A LETTER TO MY BEST FRIEND

I had a dream you came to my house and
watched me from the bottom of my stairs.
I asked what you wanted and you didn't
answer. Instead, you pulled out a bottle
of Prozac and uncapped it with steady
hands and downed the whole thing
right in front of me.

I called an ambulance but they didn't come
in time, and your last words were telling me
it was my fault. You had wanted to hurt me.
Because I am not my mother, I tried and
could not resuscitate you in time and you
died holding my hand on the steps of my
childhood home.

I don't know what this means but I worry
sometimes that my dreams are predictions.
I think I know there is nothing I can do to
stop you. Dream me couldn't wretch the
bottle from your hand and I have a feeling
the real me couldn't either.

PERTAINING TO MY INABILITY TO CONNECT WITH OTHERS (PART I)

i.
All my teeth fell out when I
wasn't looking. You searched for them
for me but found nothing. You said maybe
I swallowed them in my sleep.

ii.
I am scared of telling you the truth.
I do not know what hole I have dug for myself,
only that suffocating
and drowning
hurt the same.

iii.
Open your mouth, you said,
unclench the rusted hinge of your jaw, break
the bone if you have to, unstick your tongue
from the roof of your mouth. Heat it over a slow fire
until it melts,
until you feel yourself dripping
down your own throat and you become
candle wax,
until you wish you could stop
but cannot.

Do you remember the night
you burnt yourself?
Do you remember how you
could not move away?

iv.
You could not move away.

v.
I want to stop thinking about it but every dream I have
we are on your couch and I am laying in your lap and you
are playing with my hair and I am hurting and melting and
burning and do not show you, and you comb your hands
through my hair and do not comment on the parts of myself
you find under your nails later that afternoon, and I still wonder
if you ever saw, if you ever knew, if there was ever a part of you
that wanted to tell me it was alright, or if my melting had been
so quiet
even you had not seen.

vi.
Did you ever find my teeth?

NOVEMBER TOUR, OR:
HAPPY BIRTHDAY YOU PIECE OF SHIT

Here's the seed. Here's where I tore open my brain
to plant it. Look closely: here's the ending, the saga,
where it began. Here's where I dug my hands
into the truth and tried to pry it from my skull. Here's
where I wish the scars would heal. Here's where I don't.

Here's where my life stopped moving
in slow motion,
where I sped it up,
where I chewed anger
with my Friday brunch,
two bags of chips and coins
for 44-minute parking.
Here's where another year greets me:

happy birthday you piece of shit,
how does loneliness taste?

Here's where I tried to brush it off.
Here's where I couldn't.

Look and you'll see the past thirty-seven days
rounding a corner with a spiked baseball bat
slung over its shoulder. Slow it down,
and you'll see the moment we collide.
Speed it up again.
Here I point to October,
and he's got nothing nice to say to you.
I want to ask you to describe the aftertaste

of betrayal to me, just to make sure you swallowed it.
Here's where I smashed your fine china—
the red stains where your medicine
sat for days and days and days.
Here's where *I* took it instead;
somebody had to.

Here's where it ends,
really, actually, truly this time
or
at the very least
here is where I hope it does.

TONSILLECTOMY

i.
In the morning I poured Diet Coke for breakfast and
stood with my phone charging at the kitchen counter,
breathing life slowly back into the dead. Somewhere
in the house, you did not know anything at all yet.
Somewhere in the house you chose not to know.
The ice clattered against the plastic and this morning it
sounded like torture. Like you, in this house somewhere,
like your voice when you told me weeks and weeks later
that you didn't mean any of it.

ii.
My father asks me where it hurts and I
tell him *everywhere* because it's quickest.
I don't tell him *here,* where I expected more,
or *here,* where I expected nothing and still
had something taken from me. I don't tell him
where you prodded the wounds you were convinced
didn't exist or where your spit met my cheek.
I didn't tell him.

I want to think he would believe me, but I
have not survived these ninety-six hours
only to learn nothing.

iii.
When do you think I stopped seeing you as a goddess?
Athenian wit and Artemis fire and Hera loyalty but I
remember it withering—fading away from you.
You never seemed to notice.

iv.
I noticed.

v.
What I don't know won't hurt me but what I
find out about you later will scrape what little trust
I had left from the back of my throat and
parade my tonsils around as a trophy.
Look, this knowledge will say, *at what we have found*
and what we have turned him into. See how he
writhes and wishes to be back shrouded in
ignorance. See how he doesn't want us in his sight,

but the knowledge will not let go,
no matter how long I beg for it back.

"HOW HAVE YOU BEEN?"

I didn't wake up until four P.M. today and
that was still too early. I want to leave
behind everyone I know and move to Boston.
I want to visit Arizona and I can't stand coffee
anymore. I tried peach-flavored tea today. I
thought about peach-pits. I thought about how
much I hate them. The slices. The way you say
the words. I used to be proud of you but now
my blood just boils. I wish it wouldn't. I wear
bitterness like a coat and don't try to shrug it
off. I wish I would. But I've been shrugging off
so many things lately: The apology. The burning.
The way I can't write anymore. The way my head
spins when you talk. I want to move to Boston.
I want to try raspberry tea. I want to sleep
until my identity wears off, until my skin melts
off my body and I am nothing but muscle and blood
and bone and marrow and you have not touched me.
I want to apologize, but what else is new?
There is no adequate response,
but there are true ones. A hundred of them.
I started using different ChapStick.
I did my laundry for the first time in weeks.
I stopped drinking Diet Coke.

But I still hate how you pronounce "peaches."

MUSING IN THE
AIRPORT PARKING LOT
ROW 2F, 7:09 A.M.

There's a pounding in my head
that won't ever go away.
You tell me it can be stopped.
You tell me I'm overreacting.

I find an iron. You tell me no,
that's not what you meant.
You tell me don't worry about it,
forget it, it didn't matter.

I go down to the river but
it is flooded from rain. I
go back home but
it is flooded from grief. I

leave the house and someone
knocks on my cranium,
hello? Anyone there?
but Mama taught me not

to open the door for strangers.
For anybody. The rain floods
the whole town. Grief
floods the whole town.

I swallow pounds of Tylenol
while the rain laps at my ankles
and when the headache crescendos you
still tell me I am overreacting.

DROUGHT

You want and want
and want and want
and you have spent
so much time
telling me how it
is my fault that I
don't want to give
anyone anything
that I don't know
if that makes it
okay for you to
take it.

"DO YOU HAVE THE TIME?"

No, but I do have a bone. Here, you can pick it
yourself if it makes you more comfortable. No,
don't worry. I could never make you feel that way.
I would never. Do I have the time? No, sorry;
someone I used to know slammed my watch
into the ground. The plan was to swallow the dial
in hopes it would make them forget, they said.
I never found out if it worked or not. Did I ever
have the time? I was busy trying to forget too,
only I would startle at the wine bottle's pop
like my hands were not the ones pressing
into the cork, and I didn't have a second watch
to dismantle or a stranger's to break, so I was left
like the rest of us, left to forget, a dusty and decaying
method of waiting and watching until I thought
my body would get stuck that way.

Here's the bone. Go on. Aren't you going to pick it?
We're all watching. We're all waiting.

WALLPAPER, SHOVEL, AND KEY

The parking lot told me to face myself
and left me with a rabbit for a heart.
The problem with me is that
I have no one to turn to. The problem
with me is that I won't turn to those
I do have. The problem with me is the
shaking of my hands on the steering
wheel, the problem with me is the gas
gauge falling all the way to E, the
problem with me is that I won't
acknowledge what that stands for.

The week begins. I claim it one
of truth. I claim it one of long
showers and a rabbit locked in
the prison of my chest. I claim it
one of swallowed keys, eaten by
my own pride so I can't let my hands
shake. *Won't* let my hands shake. I
make sure my tank is full, the gauge
left on F but my friend reads it to mean
FORGET. She says, *I didn't mean it.*
I say, *It's okay,* because it is. I say,
Let's bury it. She says, *Where?* I say, *Here*
and show her the cage with my rabbit.

I hand her a shovel. We get digging.
The paint on my walls shrivels up and
threatens to fall off if I don't give
it enough attention. To the wallpaper
I say, *I'm here.* I say, *I won't go.* It
says, *no. Don't lie. All things do,*
eventually. I say, *I am not all things.*
It says, *Don't make promises you can't*
keep. We dig for so long and the walls
watch us as we work and my arms are sore
and it is Tuesday now, and the week is
one of truth but the truth
splits me open.

MISSED CALL

If I wait any longer for you to pick up I
think I'll sink straight through the floor.
The phone keeps *ringing ringing ringing*
and I keep pressing it to my ear and
if I wait any longer for you to pick up
I think you'll make the next Phineas Gage
of me. I think you'll never answer.

At noon today I watched my mother
pierce the stem of a leaf and a stranger
spill his drink on the tile. At noon
today I cried in a sandwich shop, and
thank God the stranger didn't notice.
Thank God my mother did. If this phone rings
one more time I'll hang up for good.
If this phone rings two more times I'll
hang up for good. Sorry, three's the charm.

This evening I sprawled out on my bedroom
floor. This evening anger clamped its orange-
hot body around my shoulders and said I
could let go only when you picked up, and it
is burning through fabric and flesh but

the phone is still ringing.

PART II

HOW TO TURN SOMETHING UGLY

i.
Turn the lights off. Wait for the crackling. Hear it yet? That's
the sound of a rib cage being opened, / of the lungs and all her
components deflating like a year-old balloon. If you wait / for
the puss to dissolve you'll only get blood on your fingertips / and
there it will be, stains of your thumbprints / all over the room.

ii.
Leave your headlights on. The buck is worth a fixture and a trip
to the mechanic, / but is it worth a life? Patches of fur / all over
your dashboard. The skin is the most useless part, restorable,
wasted on a beast / like this. Look at its antlers like protruding
front teeth and its hooves like overgrown nails. Its blood / will
become much more digestible this way.

iii.
Stand in front of the mirror. Middle finger and thumb against
the nose, / pull out the gunk from the pores like ripping leaves
from a tree / but don't bother counting beforehand. Look at it.
There, on your finger: microscopic dirt, grease in the holes of
you, / those openings to breathe, / like a million fish gills on your
cheeks and nose. How does it feel to be open? / Open all the time?

iv.

Do not throw the deer a wake. There are flowers left on its grave,
/ your grave, / their petals aching, / the bulbous outline like a
pustule on the chin, a blemish. A sympathetic sign, / an apology
for your loss. Do not look at the car. Its body bent / like an
acrobat's, the deer its hula hoop, / your foot on the gas a sign.

v.

Do not wait for a sign. From God, / from anyone. Because here
she will be: a splintered being, the buck / a hole in her pelt,
his absence a collection of moments. And she will not wait for
your pause, your lingering. She will only drive those overgrown
toenails into the packed-clay dirt / and here it is, that warning,
blue and red siren song / while she stomps her way to Eden.

vi.

Look at your fingers. The report papers you have smeared. The
prints you have left behind / proof / of the wake.

vii.

Listen: firecrackers in the dark.

ON: THE MADWOMAN IN THE ATTIC

There are different parts to this story:
a silver key and a windowless room;
a father who swallows pills of anger
for breakfast, dinner, and supper;
a husband who runs from love as
quickly as he falls into it.
There is a silence of fifteen years,
a festering illness, a mud-drenched bride.
There are different parts to this story, but
none of them are mine.

Mad woman, deranged woman,
hideous woman—more animal than human,
more ghost than person.
An eye for an eye
makes the whole world blind, but I
didn't want anything but freedom.
But that silver key. But a room
with a window, a husband who loves me
more than he fears me,
a life
worth living.
I didn't start out wanting fire;
I started wanting warmth.

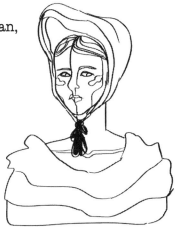

But a woman with a candle is a threat,
a woman with a temper is a threat, a woman
in pain, who speaks out on her pain,
can only bring her husband down, so

you may claim me insane, may
lock me in that room, may make
a ghost of me. But remember,
fifteen years of solitude will eat
what sanity you believed I could not possess
until I am a forest fire, until you feel my hands
around your neck even in your sleep.

So remember this,
as I will remember you,
dearest Edward,
when I am falling out that window
and Thornfield is burning
behind me.

A POEM ABOUT TODAY

Today force-fed me a rock and
it traveled down to my stomach,
but it won't dissolve.
Today woke me with stiff fingers on my lips
and said, *here*. Said, *I will be kind to you, or*
at least I will try, and I want to believe it is trying,
but my throat still burns. Today
moved my limbs. Today drove my car. Today
stopped at a red light and wished it hadn't.
In traffic, I prayed to today,
please be kind,
please be kind,
please be kind.

But my throat still burns from its knuckles
scraping against my esophagus.
I want to believe it is trying, but
my throat still burns.

SILVER SPEECH

Every time
you open your mouth
it reminds me how I am
sick of being quiet.

I
almost said something
today. I almost said
something.

ON: HOLDEN CAULFIELD'S BELIEVED DIAGNOSIS OF "JUST SOME MORE ANGSTY TEENAGE BULLSHIT"

I've been feeling it for some time now, this—
I think you call it sinking. I think you call it drowning.
I think you call it water in my lungs, but where'd the
water go? I just wanna know where it went. I just
wanna know.

So I've been feeling it for a while. So I've been feeling it,
and I don't really get how this connects: how the story
is read, how the pages keep turning, how my mouth moves
at a hundred miles an hour trying to get this all out, and
what comes through the filter to you is just noise.

I just wanna know where the water goes, how I can drown
when I'm still just sitting here talking, how I can see that body
even when I close my eyes, how the window was somehow
a million feet up from the ground, how he jumped without looking,
how he ended up brain-splattered-body-broken-on-the-concrete
-dead. Just wanna know how that isn't worth anything.

See, I've been feeling it for a while now. I've been telling you
for a while now. I'm still thinking about the scars on my hand where
they kissed glass, the broken garage door, the failing grades.

I'm still thinking about the baseball glove,
his poems, the cemetery.
Still thinking about the open window in summer,
the look in those boys' eyes,
those stupid *fucking* flowers—

Allie,
I call for you to help me but you still haven't come.

And Jane, well.
I call for her to help me but she still won't come.

You get yet why I've been feeling it?

So I'm sorry, so I'll just dance 'til I'm stupid, 'til
the window's locked and those flowers are dead, 'til
I fall out of my own skeleton and I don't have to think
about the way she looks when she thinks I love her, I
don't have to think about the cracks in the sidewalk,
don't have to think about where they end and how they end
and the fact that there was blood here where my shoe's stepping,
where I'm standing, where everyone's standing, 'til I
don't have to think about how we're all
always just standing
on some kid's
fucking
blood.

If you could,

just tell me how that isn't worth
anything.

I just wanna know.

PERTAINING TO MY INABILITY TO CONNECT WITH OTHERS (PART II)

i.
I don't know where my loyalties lie and I
think this scares you. If you had to choose,
who? If you had to pick, when? I wish
I hated you for talking about it. I wish
I didn't. I wish I didn't burn my tongue
on every truth I tasted, wish I didn't scare
so easily, wish I was more like
you you you.

I wish I didn't wake up most days wanting
to fold the photograph of my life into thumb-sized
pieces and tear through each one with the teeth
you want me to make into scissors.

If you had to guess,
when did it start? If you had to say,
where did you learn it from?

I cannot tell you;
I was never given the answer.

ii.
I think I was taught this language when I was
still in the womb.

iii.
There is no easy way to say this except flat out:
these feelings are not pretty.
I wish they were peach slices,

or bare feet up hills,

or the glossy version of two A.M.

But I saw a girl today with bags under her eyes so heavy
it looked like she hadn't slept in decades;

and the first memory I have of cutting fruit is
my grandmother nearly slicing her finger off;

and the last time I ran bare-foot up a hill I was
running
from something.

iv.
Do they need to be pretty?
Can they not just *be*?

v.
How can you beg me for the truth and not flinch
when I spit gasoline opening my mouth? How
can you speak so easily? How can anyone say,
here,
I will point you to my Achilles heel
and hand you my bow
and you will hand me yours?

Sometimes I think we're too different to last much longer.
Sometimes I wonder how we have even gotten this far.

vi.
I wish I didn't flinch.

ON: ENKIDU'S "BECOMING"

I remember it now. The blade of her
scissors. The strands of hair sticking
to my neck as they fell. I've never
been scared of anything. But she,
with her long legs, carrying the scent
of fruit and human,
cut my hair.
We made you human, they said. *We made*
you a man.
But I was a man before she touched me,
and no one asked if this was **what I wanted.**
This was never what I
wanted.

But I live on,
scalp shaven,
and they say that,
now,
I am clean.

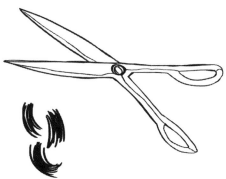

I wonder what it was that made me
dirty.

IN DEFENSE OF THE CLOSET

i.
Why do you ask me to pour out my entrails?
Why am I expected to hand my lungs
and beating heart over for others to examine?
Why must I give you a piece of myself
without knowing for sure that you will give it back?
That you won't look at my lungs barely
filling with air and wrap a fist around
their diameter until the world becomes only
the stars behind my eyelids when I'm sleeping?
How do I know you won't pierce the tissue
of my eardrums with regurgitated fallacies
until they burst like balloons? How do I know
you will not see how rapidly my heart beats
in your open palm and decide it has done
enough beating? Why must I make myself vulnerable
if you will tell me nothing of equal value in return?
If the only response you have will be to ask
what my parents think?
Ask how long I have known?
Ask when I will decide it is enough?

ii.
The stories of people like me are short
and sad
and lonely
and harsh
and I have seen what people like me receive
when they are not careful.

When they refuse the camouflage
that comes so second nature for some of us.
I have seen how unforgiving
those around us are of deviations;
of tells; of perceived
weakness.

iii.
When Icarus fell in love with the sun, Apollo
didn't bat an eye, but the moment his love
overtook him he was thrown back to earth
with sunburnt cheeks and chapped lips, and
before he hit the ground, the wax burnt
feathers into his shoulder
blades
and the gods
only
watched
and we are told this is
hubris;
we are told this is
the fall of Icarus,
his
punishment
for
pride.

iv.
Silence
does not mean denial
and for some of us
a quiet existence
is better than
none at all.

v.
The price of Milk's life was
seven years for a politician
and Charlie Howard offered them his lungs
and they said he was finished breathing
and Nireah Johnson's body was made
into a pillar of fire to keep her murderer warm
and Lawrence King didn't live long enough
to learn how to drive and
Mark Carson didn't answer whether
or not he wanted to die because
they'd already answered for him
and forty-nine souls who were in
the wrong place
at the wrong time
didn't leave that club that night
and the world decided
these cases were worth less
than a Bible verse
in the local newspaper.

vi.
Trust me when I say
I do not want to be scared
of living either.

PORTRAIT OF A YOUNG MAN

I wonder how long it will take
until the knocking in my head crescendos,
until the lie has been repeated so often
that it becomes a sort of truth.
I wonder who was the first person
to make me this way—
who first looked at me and said
you are wrong; who first stripped my identity,
plunged shit-covered hands into its meat
and dug around for its vitals, its cavities,
its emptiness and, upon realizing
there is no place of me left uncovered,
removed their bare fingers and
claimed it was me
who infected
them.

I wonder who first decided I do not have
the final say on my sense of self. Who
decided I was only sick?
Who wrote the guidelines for this infection,
and who allowed them to throw me in for
fixing?

Who decides
what needs fixing?

You tell me that the TV is a good place to start.
So I ask you: who decided I have no place with others,
or, if I do,
only to play the role of villain or body bag?
Is my death so funny that you must plaster it on
your LCD screens for every man and woman and
impressionable child to lap up and laugh at?
Do you know your words' weights, their bite?
Do you notice it at all?
Or will you tell me your laughing
is only with good intentions?

You wonder why I am not laughing,
so I will tell you this:

My viscera are still healing from your invasive
surgery, and even now my body remembers
the pain your gloveless hands caused,
and the knocking in my head has
not stopped, but because of
you I have forgotten
who started
it.

FISH

The other day someone told me I was
gutting myself as if fitting puzzle pieces together
counts as mutilation.
They asked me what went next,
what part of myself I
was planning to rip off after this.
Next thing you know
they'll be getting surgeries to become animals.
Fallacies fall from strangers' mouths like raindrops
and become a heavy downpour when I'm alone.

It is less like this with others,
but I read a book two years ago that compared me
to a parrotfish.
I'm still deciding if that is another fallacy,
and if it is,
if it makes it any better
that there are good intentions.

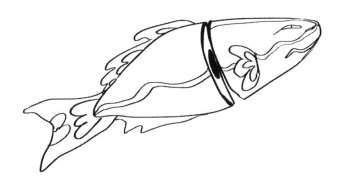

I GO TO THE MOVIES WITH A BOY

for the first time and I think
the world might collapse into itself.
We stand in the concession line and my
fingertips tremble with something—
a desire for touch / and a fear for it,
the lingering stare of the audience,
the performance I am always putting / on

because yes, here we are,
and I tug at my button down and wonder
if the whole town can tell what I am / what
we are and if so, if there is anybody
here who cares enough to do something
about it.

So we stand there. So we're breathing,
and the line creeps ever forward. My hand
is so much smaller in this moment than I
want it to be / need it to be;

if I clenched it in a fist would that
keep away the violence?

Yes, maybe,
or no, possibly,
or I will hope I do not have to find out but I
am finding out the other parts:

how the fist keeps him from reaching for me,
how he might know what I am thinking or maybe
think it too;

and oh, how we stand with our arms at our sides,
afraid for / of / one another and the weight of touch;

how the distance between our shoulders is so far,
and I am only thinking the entire time
they must know, they must know;

and every face I pass is a potential instigator,
a bible verse with consonants that sound
like gunshots / blessings that become an AR-556
the moment I turn my head and there are so many
that I fear chewing through the bullets.

So I lose the touch / so I don't look around,
and the line moves up another foot and I
tug at my button down and wait
for the three words—six / if you have the patience—

the same way I am still waiting for hell fire to rain down
and drench me for my sins, sear away my skin and bones until
it is just the treading part of me—

and our hands sway at our sides, palm
trees in a storm, silent casualties of a culture
that forces a clenched fist. We say nothing,

and my fingertips are
still trembling.

A LETTER TO THE GIRLS
WHO THEY SAY CONVERTED ME

The womb of your life is vacant
but I still think about you every now and then.
You pressed a sweaty palm to my own
while a stoner breathed smoke over my other shoulder.
In an empty theater only four
sat in the audience and she
told me her name was Natalia.
Her womb was not a womb but a
battleground; a heaven; a plight.
You,
clumsy in your speech and frightened in your flirting,
asked me why I never said anything back.
I told you I wasn't sure but not
that I never would be.

You never did get to tell me your name
but I read it sometimes,
from friends,
blinking back at me from the cracked screen of my phone,
telling me you have *changed her name to Daniella*
and I do not miss the change in pronouns, either.

I still wonder how you're doing.

A LETTER TO THE BOY ON SCHOOL BUS #35 WHO THE OTHER KIDS CALLED "FAG"

I don't know how to erase the graffiti on your memories but
if I could I would scrub them clean. I don't know why I said nothing.
I don't know why I brushed past you in the aisle and pretended I
hadn't met your eyes. I don't know why I never checked up on you.
I watched the kids our age grin as you sat down, hurl hand grenades
of three-plus-letter-slurs towards your seat and laugh when you choked
on the smoke. I watched you learn not to breathe, not to let them know,
watched as you started learning to throw the grenades right back.
FAG and *GAY* and *COCKSUCKER* were eventually scarred into the bus's
seats—all of them—and they scarred there, too, somewhere on you.
I never told any of those kids how you asked me out years later,
how you dyed your hair purple and showed up to GSA.

Even now I don't ask about that bus,
about the eleven-year-old hunched over in his seat, alone, head
lowered, backpack on, ready to escape the moment the bombs
started to go off
again.

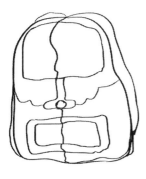

ODE TO MY CAR

The city has never looked so desolate.
The street is vacant like the Rapture has come
and I am the only one left on our earth.

I am pressing on the gas and you move me forward.
I am pressing on the brakes and you stop before we
cross into the intersection. There is nobody here

but I want to say thank you. For all the times I have
thought about slamming us into a building, about
jerking the wheel too sharply to the left, too quickly;

for all the times I have been afraid to start the engine
because of what I know could happen, what I know I
sometimes wish would happen—for all those times I

still make it home safe. You still get me home safe.
With a broken turn signal and two-hundred thousand miles
on you, you still get me home safe. Despite the odds,

you are the most secure staple in my life. During this Rapture,
when my head is whirling, when I have entered a shift
for the third time in my life, you still get me home. You,

you, who I have dreaded, who I have imagined as a tool
for my own inevitable disaster, who I have avoided for fear
of one day going through with it, who I have neglected and

abused and been ungrateful for—against all odds,
against everything I have done and said, against the whole
world telling me I should not be alive right now—

you

still get me home safe.

I WANT TO WRITE IN MEMORIES (PART II)

I will never
be able to get
it all down and
I'm still learning
how to be okay
with that.

CROWBAR

Did you know you would respond like that?
The sidewalk you disappeared down still smells
like cigarettes. The floorboards they slithered under
never came up because we still never found a crowbar
big enough to tear them from their roots.

I'm sorry. I didn't mean it. None of us meant it.
How else could you have responded?
Sometimes when you're not doing well you think
about the paper between your fingers and the rot
in your teeth, but it is never for the right reasons.
Sometimes you remember the field they decayed in,
three years too late.

Do you remember? The house you grew up in?
The trees you left the box sleeping under?
Like clockwork, you return to that field
in hopes that they have survived the bite of time,
somehow.

Yes, you'll remember now; this is why you
responded the way that you did; why it hurt so
much when it hurts others so little. Some things
can never be regained once lost—and when gained,
can never leave you, no matter how much
you wish they would.

Will it ever unstick? Will the rot ever go away?

I THOUGHT I SAW YOU IN A GROCERY STORE PARKING LOT

In the dairy aisle I stood with my arms outstretched
waiting   for you to come to me   like I
always do when I'm alone, the handle of the shopping
cart pressed into me, but it felt like a   crater
rocking the earth,   the same crater that rocked our
earth twenty some years ago when you were born
because your birth made even God weep,   but I
can't stop thinking how this is the worst part, that
I can't remember how old you are,   that I don't
need to remember how old you are, that I choose
to stand   in front of the half-off yogurt because
I can't stop thinking   hoping   the person I saw
in the parking lot is still there, is somehow you, and
I stay   standing there   and waiting
to hear the doors of the store slide open and the ground
crack   under my feet, you   returned
to us like the messiah, but it has been way more than
two days now and   I've never been much of a believer
and   the ice cream in my cart is   starting to
melt   and the ice cream in my cart is   starting to
melt   and I know the parking lot is empty now
so I think I should just   grab the yogurt
and go.

A LETTER TO THE SISTER
FROM THE LITTLE BROTHER

I want to write you a poem—
one for each day you've been gone.
For years now I have been trying,
but the days escape me and I am left
chasing the tail of this stubborn rabbit,
always out of reach, always just a little
too far away.

Did you know flowers could wilt that quickly?
I didn't. Maybe that's why Mom buys them plastic.
Did you know I made a mistake the other day?
Did I tell you about the morning I woke up
with so much guilt in my stomach I
would've rather died?
Did I tell you how we're doing?

I want
to write you a poem
for every day you've been gone
but it has been close to a thousand now
and I can only write so many before I think my bones
will melt under the pressure of my heart, until I think
my lungs will puncture with the force I am using
just so they will fill.

Nothing compares to talking
but even if you can't respond I
will write your side of the dialogue—

or—at least—
I will go crazy trying to.

A THANK YOU LETTER
FROM THE YOUNGEST CHILD
TO THE MIDDLE

The day the police knocked on our door, you pushed
your stuffed animals off the side of your bed and made
room for me. You folded onto the carpet
and didn't get up.
Your shoulders shook like the pounding
on our door had caused an earthquake,
like the demands to open up had ripped
your spine out through your throat
and even then you told me things would be
okay.

The difference between my body and yours was that
you didn't collapse,
even when you collapsed—
was that you held
me the whole night and told me not to worry,
and didn't point out
that your hands were shaking, too.

The difference was that you panicked when I wasn't home
on time, when I stayed with my bedroom door locked,
when I went swimming with you those summers
with a hundred still-healing scars on my thighs—
but you just dialed my number and spoke with an even voice;
you knocked on my door and asked me to come out;
you just
kept swimming.

The difference between my body and yours was that
I didn't know you were worried, you were scared,
until years later, when I told you I no longer wanted to die,
and you pulled me into you and told me how relieved you were,
how scary it was to come home every day fearing that you'd find
     my body
hanging
somewhere in the house.

The difference was that when the police came I
laid on your bed while the shadows danced
in the hallway outside your room. The difference is that
you loved me enough to make room for my
eight-year-old body
when there was
never even
enough
for
yours.

ROADKILL

My mother pulls over for a monochrome corpse,
puts the car in park and chances running into the road
for a signal,
a black and white star,
someone's love.
It is still warm when she picks it up and holds its body
just long enough to place it somewhere
safe—or,
safer,
because the damage has been done.
She is warm but never breathing,
a blood-letting,
a comet of grief.

I pretend,
not for the first time,
not to notice my mother cry.

HOME, BEFORE

The gravel crunches under a car's wheels:
one, two, three, four pairs of them, each
stopping and going like they're afraid
to stay here too long.   In the kitchen,
my father makes spaghetti for dinner, no
meatballs, and my best friend asks if he
can heat some up for himself.   The curtains
are drawn and my grandmother loses her
hair curlers again. The Christmas tree
falls over for the second time
that year.   *Come closer*, she mumbles
into my sister's ear, *I have something to tell you*
and slips her a five-dollar bill.   The other sister
smokes on the patio for the fourth time today,
one, two, three, four while her friends come
and go from our driveway.   That year
her boyfriend rides my bike off the roof
of our house into the pool, and my mother
treats them to silence for dinner. No spaghetti for them
but sweet tea will always be waiting when
they come home,   no matter how
many cigarettes she smokes. My dad says my mom
has too soft a heart. My sister says my dad will find
that his own viscera are just as exposed.
And   he does.

ALBINO

My mother wakes me up just as the sky,
dark with night, begins to undress
shyly into morning. Wrapped in her bathrobe
she tells me to get my camera and points me towards
the patio door, where morning mist still lays
over our yard like a second skin.
In the distance, there is
the white glow of a deer
—lonely.
My mother tells me in a quiet voice
about her father, how as a child she cried
when he left for hunting trips,
how she prayed he would not find
any deer to shoot.
And she points to this one
with its glowing
and we are both thinking about our neighbor with his guns
and the deer heads hung on my aunt's walls
and the light as it is coming over the horizon.
And she tells me that she feels
still
like a child.

BRICKS

You do not know it now
but this will be your biggest memory.
You do not catalogue the dog-eared pages
of her journal, the ink scribbles smudged
on every page, her smell, smoke with summer
with old perfume; you do not realize how
much space these things will take. You do not
know that the way you stare at the bricks,
or the way she pulls her robe around her tighter,
or the uncomfortable way you sit will become
a prayer one day, a plea, some kind of
refuge.

Right now,
all you know
is that it is near midnight,
and your sister asks to take a break
from the movie so she can smoke.

All you know is
that cigarette,
the glowing down.

A LETTER TO THE READER

If you're interested, here's some background information that might help you understand these poems more:

I. When I was fourteen years old, my oldest sister passed away.

  i. It was sudden. Unexpected. She was eleven years older than me. Still is, I suppose. That's one of those things about death—it makes everything blurry. Screws with even the facts you believed were undeniable.

  ii. I have another sister, only two years older than me, and my oldest sister had a daughter before she passed. I talk about all three of them in these poems.

II. Six months before my sister passed, I came out to my family as transgender.

  i. Specifically, trans male. During middle school, I knew there was a disconnect between my mind and body, but it wasn't until I met a trans girl at a summer camp that I truly understood.

  ii. At the end of eighth grade, I came out to my mother. The same day, she and I decided on my new name: Gray.

    a. It's my middle name. I wanted to go by Michael, but Gray was an option with a safety net built in. When I went to high school in the fall, I could deflect transphobia with the excuse that it was my middle name. So, I agreed. Although my legal name is now changed to Michael Gray, I still prefer Gray.

III. I wrote the majority of these poems when my grief was still all consuming, back when I thought that if I did not write about it, I might die.

   i.   Years later, I still think I might've. Maybe it sounds silly, but sometimes I think writing saved me. It didn't bring my sister back, but it let me talk and breathe and sit and think and talk and breathe again. Writing is the only thing I have ever done that has felt, to me, undeniably important. Irreplaceable. I have always loved writing, but it wasn't until my sister passed that I realized fiction was not enough for me; I needed *poetry*.

   ii.   But I did not go looking for poetry—I stumbled upon it. My freshman English class did a unit on poetry. We were required to write for a slam, and the class would vote on who to send to the next level. My poem— a flimsy attempt at mimicking the beautiful pieces I had seen performed on YouTube weeks before in preparation—was selected to head to the next round. I wasn't chosen after that, but I didn't care. I had created something.

   iii. I transferred to an arts school the following year. There, I wrote some more poetry, but I focused mostly on fiction and my goals of being a novelist; even though the words were bubbling out my throat, I was scared to get them started. Who would want to read these? Who would want to listen?

    iv.   Then, Southern Word came to my school.

          a.   Southern Word is an organization that goes around to schools and teaches kids through poetry. Among other things, they do slams, workshops, and The Nashville Youth Poet Laureate program, where one teenage poet is chosen to represent Nashville's youth and go around the city, writing and performing and inspiring. My teacher invited every student to apply, so I did.

    v.   I won.

    vi.   I could not be more grateful to Southern Word for this opportunity. For this community. For this experience. It's been invaluable. Irreplaceable.

IV. I am still healing. I am still hurting. It has been years since my sister passed, but I don't know that I will ever "get over" it. These poems helped, I think. They helped get it out. They helped keep me alive. They helped me believe I could make something to help others. But they are not a substitute for what happened.

V. If you are hurting—if you are healing—if you've lost someone, to death or time or circumstance—if you've ever been ill or have ever been "other"—I hope you found something in this book that you connect with. Something that gives you room to talk and breathe and sit and think and talk and breathe again.

ACKNOWLEDGMENTS

This book was a labor of love, a creature of grief, an evidence of healing. These poems—and my journey to them—could not have been possible without the following:

I. My mother and father and their indispensable love and support.

    i. Many other parents would have—and often do—fold under the pressure of supporting such a troubled teen. But neither of you ever gave up on me. You never shut me down. You never tried to tell me I was anything but what I am, even when I didn't fully know what that was yet. And for that, I can never thank you enough.

II. The middle child, Marcie.

    i. I already wrote you a thank you letter, but here's another one: thank you thank you thank you! For rooming with me, for believing in me, for caring for me. For being there. And also, for letting me annoy your cat. :)

III. The niece/little sister, Lani.

    i. You're not old enough yet to be allowed to read these poems, and that's totally okay. But you will be someday, and I want you to know, whenever that day comes, how much I love you and how much you mean to me and how proud I always am of you.

IV. The editor and mentor and friend, Kelly.

    i. I can't thank you enough for your help with these poems.

Having someone there to guide and encourage me,
especially someone as kind and talented as you are,
is ninety percent of why these poems are in the shape
they are. I can't tell you how much it helped me,
knowing there was another poet looking at my work and
believing I could come out the other end with a book.
That's not an easy job. Thank you.

V. The childhood best friend.

    i. I can't imagine living a life without you in it. When
there was nobody else to love me, nobody else to call,
you were always there. Your friendship has been a
greater comfort to me than you can ever imagine, and
your understanding and love and support has yet to be
rivaled. Ten years, baby. A whole-ass decade, and I love
you just as much. Here's to many more years losing our
voices signing along in the car and driving to get fast
food at two A.M. and crying on our couches and playing
Just Dance and taking horrible selfies and friendship,
friendship, friendship.

VI. The friend group I never realized I needed.

    i. What more can I say? You three were there when I had
little else to turn to. You were there to prove life wrong.
You were there to introduce me to fun again! To staying
up late on a phone call! To watching old TV shows
together! To flying out across the country by myself just
to see you guys! All three of you are so, so important to
me. Thank you for letting me be a part of your lives, and
for being a part of mine.

VII. The program, Southern Word.

    i. Just to reiterate: none of this could have been possible without Southern Word's generosity and belief in me and encouragement. The community Southern Word has provided has truly changed my life. And thank you, Ben, for not giving up on this project.

VIII. The publisher, Flowerpot Press.

    i. Like Southern Word, this wouldn't be possible without Flowerpot Press. Thank you guys so, so much for your help and your interest and your involvement in this project. I can't express how much it means to me.

IX. The reader—you!

    i. If you've gotten this far—if you've picked up the book at all—thank you, thank you, thank you, thank you.

ABOUT THE AUTHOR

Michael Gray Bulla is a writer and poet from Franklin, Tennessee. As well as being the 2017 Nashville Youth Poet Laureate, he has won six awards from the Scholastic Art and Writing competition in the Short Story, Science Fiction & Fantasy, and Flash Fiction categories. He is a graduate from Nashville School of the Arts and is pursuing an English degree at Wells College. During the rare moments when he isn't writing, he can be found drawing, consuming copious amounts of Diet Coke, or watching 90s cartoons with his niece. LETTERS TO THE HOME is his first poetry collection.